Essential Question
How do traditions connect people?

A Song for Marie and Ajidamo

by Marcie Rendon
White Earth Anishinabe

illustrated by Val Paul Taylor

Chapter 1 Change

Marie swung the bucket back and forth as she walked down the gravel road. Fine sand-colored dust clung to her bare feet. Crickets chirped in the ditches, a melody of summertime heat. A few monarch butterflies hovered over the milkweeds lining the road. Marie remembered that her grandmother had told her she would find the chokecherry bushes at the quarter-mile corner south of the village.

She glanced at the Episcopalian church as she walked by. "Nin dah zhe be koom, Je sus, Kah zhe shin suh ke yuh win." The words floated on the hot summer air. Grandma and Grandpa were always speaking Ojibwe, especially when they didn't want her to know what they were talking about. Marie understood way more Ojibwe than she let on. Nin dah zhe be koom …. The song faded as Marie walked farther down the road.

Grandma never went to church and often grumbled about the "white man's religion." These days, Grandma grumbled about a lot of things, including some "relocation plan" the government had for Indians. Last night Marie overheard Grandma, Grandpa, and Uncle Ajidamo talking late into the night. Grandma had made it clear she despised the government's new program.

Grandma was the only one in Pine Bend, Minnesota, to have a television. So everyone from six houses around crowded into Grandma's living room to watch the evening news. Marie sat on the floor and watched pictures of city life flash across the screen.

The city had big brick buildings, nothing like the wood houses in Pine Bend. It had paved streets and sidewalks instead of gravel roads. City women wore high heels and dresses. Men wore black suits and black ties. Marie looked at her grandmother in her long cotton dress with a blue apron tied over it. Marie tried to imagine Grandma wearing high heels instead of beaded leather moccasins. She started laughing at her own thoughts. Grandma asked, "What?"

"Nothing," Marie said, smiling. Then she looked at Grandpa in his denim overalls and his work boots. He always looked as if he was heading off to logging camp. Marie started laughing to herself all over again, imagining Grandpa wearing a suit.

Alfred Jr., who lived in the blue house, was talking to Marie's uncle, Ajidamo.

"First the government puts us on these reservations. Now, in 1956 they suddenly change their minds and want to send us to the city to build skyscrapers," he said.

Marie asked, "What's a skyscraper?"

"A building so tall it pulls the clouds right out of the sky," Ajidamo explained. Marie could tell by his laugh that he was teasing her.

Alfred Jr. laughed with him adding, "Skyscrapers are buildings taller than any of the jack pines around here. I am going to take your uncle to Zhi-gaag-go." Marie wondered if the people of Chicago knew it meant "skunk" in Ojibwe. "We'll be ironworkers, climbing to the sky to build the city. That is, if your uncle doesn't get dizzy and come right back home."

"No," corrected Ajidamo. "You're the one who's afraid to climb tall trees here when we are out logging."

The other men were also talking in excited tones about moving to Zhi-gaag-go.

While they talked, Marie imagined Uncle Ajidamo in the city. With his slicked back hair, she could easily see him striding down the sidewalk wearing a suit and tie.

Chapter 2 The Discussion

After everyone went home to bed, Grandma and Grandpa sat at the kitchen table talking in Ojibwe. They were talking about Uncle Ajidamo, even though he was sitting right there at the kitchen table with them drinking coffee. Ajidamo had turned 18 two weeks ago. The men had teased him about being too young to go to Zhi-gaag-go. He had shrugged and said, "We'll see." Now he sat at the table drinking coffee while Grandma and Grandpa threw Ojibwe words around in the air like popcorn. Ajidamo would take a sip of coffee while looking at Grandma. Another sip and look at Grandpa. Marie busied herself with a coloring book on the kitchen floor. As long as she kept quiet Grandma wouldn't tell her to go to bed.

Grandma wanted Ajidamo to stay on the reservation and be a logger. She spoke with intensity. Words flew from her mouth, and her hands spoke even faster. Grandpa mostly nodded. Whenever he tried to speak, Grandma would interrupt him and say, "The city is no place for our people."

Ajidamo finally asked loudly in English, "What about what I want to do? Climbing jack pines and cutting down 1000-pound trees can't be any less dangerous or require more endurance than climbing buildings and riveting steel."

Grandma answered, "We don't belong in the city ...." Catching sight of Marie, she said, "Get to bed, Marie."

Lying in bed, Marie slid her hand over the soft quilt that covered the drum next to her bed. The drum had been in her room, protected by the quilt, for as long as Marie could remember. She had stopped asking why the drum was there. She fell asleep listening to voices raised, voices hushed, sometimes in English, sometimes in Ojibwe. The drum vibrated slightly under her hand with the rise and fall of their voices. It lulled Marie to sleep.

Chapter 3 A Song

The next morning was Sunday. Long before the church bell rang, Grandma woke the entire village by singing at the drum, out on the gravel driveway in front of the house. Marie jumped out of bed and ran to the screen door. The sun was barely up and there was Grandma, singing at the drum, which had always been in Marie's bedroom. Grandma was singing in Ojibwe at the top of her lungs. Marie stood in the doorway, shocked. She looked up at Ajidamo as he joined her, his hair still mussed from sleep. Marie looked over her shoulder into the kitchen. Grandpa was there calmly drinking a cup of coffee.

Marie looked more closely at Grandma and the drum. She had never seen her singing at the drum before. It was sitting on a wooden pedestal with four wooden braces holding it up. Marie could see drawings on the side of the drum—one was a red hand, the other a stick figure with lightning coming from its head. Grandma used a rawhide-covered drumstick to beat out the rhythm of the song as she sang.

Marie could see faces peeking out from the windows of some of the other houses. Some men and women were standing in their doorways. The sun was just peeking through the jack pines to the east.

Grandma ended the song by shouting, "Aiii iiii iiii …," the sound rolling from the back of her throat over her tongue and out into the never-ending sky. Several of the older women standing in their doorways joined her. "Aiii iiii iiiii …" rose throughout the village.

At the end of the song, Grandma carried the drum gently to the house and asked Ajidamo to hold it for a minute. Then she went back and folded up the pieces of wood that made the pedestal. She carried it back into Marie's bedroom, with Ajidamo and the drum following her. Grandma motioned for Ajidamo and Marie to follow her back to the kitchen and sit at the table. Then she sat down next to Grandpa.

"Did you know it's against the law for me to sing at that drum? Practicing our religion, our way of life, was outlawed by the federal Civilization Regulations of 1882. I could go to prison for 30 years just for singing that song," Grandma said.

Chapter 4 The Old Ways

"Thirty years for praying our way, in our language, with our ancestors' songs. There've been nights that the drum has asked me to sing our songs. But I was afraid. I'm not afraid anymore. Let them come take me," Grandma said fiercely.

"No," squeaked out Marie.

Grandpa laughed. "She's not going anywhere," he said as he got up to answer a soft knock at the door. He returned carrying a folded piece of fabric and handed it to Grandma. "Jigs says, 'Miigwetch'."

Throughout the rest of breakfast folks from the village stopped by and gave Grandma homemade jam, fabric, and dishtowels. Grandpa put all the gifts in front of Grandma.

"Our old ways are powerful. That's why the government outlawed our traditional ways. But I sang this morning so you," said Grandma looking at Ajidamo, "can go to the big city to be an ironworker. When you go, remember this song, our language, our ways. Honor them and take them with you. Sing them from those buildings touching the sky, and we will hear them back here on the reservation."

"What do you mean?" asked Marie.

"We are always Ojibwe, always Anishinabe, whether here or in the city. This is our land. The wind knows our songs. I hear they also call Zhi-gaag-go the Windy City," Grandma chuckled. "So Ajidamo will hear me sing on the wind, just as I will hear him sing in Zhi-gaag-go." Grandma went on, "If we practice our traditional ways, we'll be strong as a people. We have retreated far enough here on the reservation. Now is the time to be a part of that big world out there. If we keep our traditions alive, we will always remember what makes us Anishinabe. It's time that I taught you both the old ways."

Marie and Ajidamo looked at each other.

Grandma smiled. "This afternoon we'll have a feast for our friends to thank them for their gifts. Marie, I want you to pick a bucket of chokecherries and I'll make chokecherry juice."

Marie looked at Grandma over her milk glass, eyebrows raised like question marks.

Grandma said, "Don't look at me like that. It's irritating. Chokecherries are one of our sacred foods."

"We've never heard you talk about this stuff before," said Marie.

"Well, enough of being silent. You need to learn our ways, especially if your uncle is going to Zhi-gaag-go to climb iron trees," she said, handing Marie the bucket.

The bushes at the quarter-mile bend in the road hung heavy with deep purple chokecherries. Marie ate a handful. The taste puckered her mouth. She found the taste almost like eating a lemon, but then the sweetness of the berries overcame the bitterness. She spit the seeds out on the ground. The tall grass made her legs itch as the sun warmed her shoulders. She could hear the wind rustle the leaves of the poplar trees.

As Marie picked berries, she thought about her grandma daring to play the drum and sing. She thought of Uncle Ajidamo and hoped he would come home wearing a suit like the men on TV. When the bucket was full, she retraced her steps back to the village. A little way past the church, she saw Grandma walking to meet her.

Grandma took the bucket from her and put her arm across Marie's shoulder. She sang softly the song she had sung on the drum that morning.

By the time they reached home, Marie thought maybe she might know how to sing the song herself.

Summarize

Use the most important details from *A Song for Marie and Ajidamo* to summarize the story. Your graphic organizer may help you.

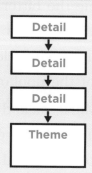

Detail
↓
Detail
↓
Detail
↓
Theme

Text Evidence

1. How is this story an example of historical fiction? GENRE

2. Why does Grandma decide to teach Marie and Ajidamo the Ojibwe traditions? THEME

3. On page 6, Marie imagines Ajidamo with "slicked back hair" and "striding down the sidewalk." What are the denotations of *slick* and *stride*? What are their connotations? CONNOTATION AND DENOTATION

4. How does Grandma change from the beginning of the story to the end of the story? WRITE ABOUT READING

Compare Texts

Read about laws throughout U.S. history that have denied Native Americans religious freedom and other basic rights.

The Civilization Regulations

In 1868, President Ulysses Grant established the "Peace Policy." Through it, the United States government made a way for Christians to set up churches on American Indian reservations. The new policy opened the way for The Civilization Regulations of 1882. These Regulations took away Native peoples' rights to practice their spiritual ways. Native Americans could face up to thirty years in prison just for praying or visiting a sacred site. On some reservations, Native people practiced their ways in secret. On other reservations, those ways were kept alive only in the memories and stories of the elders. Finally, in 1978, President Jimmy Carter signed the American Indian Religious Freedom Act into law. After this Act was signed, Native Americans were again allowed to openly practice their religions.

Native Americans gathered to sing, dance, and drum at the 39th annual Lac Courte Orielles Ojibwe "Honor the Earth" Pow Wow.

Keith Crowley/Alamy

17

The Indian Relocation Act

In the 1950s the Indian Relocation Act was passed in an effort to move Native people off the reservations to major cities like Chicago. The government wanted Native Americans to become more "American" and forfeit their traditions. The Bureau of Indian Affairs sent their agents to reservations all over the country to persuade Native Americans to move to cities. These agents handed out flyers with pictures of parks, schools, and nice homes. They also promised good jobs in construction.

Relocation offices were set up in the cities by the Bureau of Indian Affairs. These offices promised to provide training, jobs, and money to newly relocated Native Americans. Many of these promises were not kept. For many people, moving from a rural area full of family and friends to an urban area full of strangers was very difficult.

Native Americans work on a construction site in the 1950s.

A young group of Native American dancers wait to perform at the American Indian Center in Chicago.

Chicago was one of the main relocation cities. In 1953, a group of Chicago Native Americans saw the need for a multi-tribal community center. They wanted a place that would provide help and support to all the Native people who were arriving in the city. So, they started The American Indian Center which is still operating today.

Make Connections

Why did Native Americans in Chicago start a community center in the 1950s? Why was it important for Native Americans in the city to have a place to gather? ESSENTIAL QUESTION

What effect does the Indian Relocation Act have on Marie's community? TEXT TO TEXT

Focus on Genre

Historical Fiction Historical fiction tells a story that is set in the past. It often gives information about a real event and can show real people who were living at the time. Historical fiction gives the reader an understanding of life in the past.

Read and Find A *Song for Marie and Ajidamo* is based on real events and issues facing Native American communities in the 1950s. It shows how the Ojibwe worked to maintain their traditions despite the U.S. government's attempts to make them move to cities. The characters in the story are made up, but the story is inspired by fact.

Your Turn

Native Americans have a tradition of oral storytelling. The stories teach about the past.

Choose a person or an event in your family that you could tell a story about. You can make up some details to add interest, but base your story on facts. Practice telling your story until it sounds and feels right and then share it with others in your group or class.